Music by Richard Rodgers
Lyrics by Sheldon Harnick

REX logo created by Gilbert Lesser

ISBN 0-634-06711-7

WILLIAMSON MUSIC®

A RODGERS AND HAMMERSTEIN COMPANY

www.williamsonmusic.com

Exclusively Distributed By

HAL•LEONARD®
CORPORATION

7777 W. BLUEMOUND RD. P.O. BOX 13819 MILWAUKEE, WI 53213

Visit Hal Leonard Online at
www.halleonard.com

CONTENTS

*Note: "The Pears of Anjou" and "Tell Me"
were written for the original Broadway production
of REX but were cut before the New York opening.*

INTRODUCTION

REX almost ended before it began. One terrible morning, Richard Adler (one of our producers) called to tell me that Richard Rodgers had been rushed to the hospital with cancer of the larynx. My heart sank. I had not yet had the chance to get to know him, much less work with him. How could REX possibly go forward?

I hadn't reckoned with Rodgers' courage and determination. After his laryngectomy, he promptly began the difficult task of learning laryngeal speech. He worked at it resolutely and eventually mastered it. REX went forward. I found myself working with a man who had had a stroke, a heart attack, cancer of the jaw and cancer of the larynx. I came to admire and then to love him for his gallant spirit, his determination to keep going, no matter what.

We went into rehearsal with a clear idea of the story we wanted to tell. Then, as happens all too frequently, we lost our perspective. The producers, the director, the bookwriter (Sherman Yellen), Richard Rodgers and I all lost sight of the point the show was making. When REX opened on Broadway in 1976, the show seemed bogged down in historical detail and lacked a clear, straightforward narrative structure. REX had a disappointingly brief run.

Now, skip forward a quarter of a century. Sherman Yellen and I accept James Morgan's offer to present REX in his "Musicals in Mufti" series at the York Theatre Company (no sets, no costumes, small cast, music stands and a piano). When we look at the script, after our twenty-five year vacation away from it, our blunders become painfully clear. With the help of our new director, Jay Binder, we make sweeping cuts, add the transitions and connective passages we had neglected to provide before, and clarify the narrative structure. By reshaping some of the scenes, we are even able to restore some of the songs we had cut too quickly the first time around, including "Tell Me" and "The Pears of Anjou."

When the new REX was unveiled in the spring of 2001, we were delighted to see that it was (finally!) the show we had originally envisioned. This was triumphantly corroborated in 2002, when Micheal Anders presented REX (as part of a Rodgers centennial tribute) at the University of Findlay, this time with a large cast, regal sets, magnificent costumes and full orchestra. Oh, how I wish Dick Rodgers had been there to hear the response his music elicited from our enthusiastic audiences. Well, maybe he *was* there, smiling down at us from Songwriters' Heaven, saying, "See! I told you it was a good show!"

—Sheldon Harnick

AS ONCE I LOVED YOU

Lyrics by SHELDON HARNICK

Music by RICHARD RODGERS

Molto moderato

Do you re-mem-ber the morn-ing we were wed? _____
How man-y times have you rest-ed in my arms? _____

Pic-ture your-self in the chap-el once a-
How man-y nights was I there when you were

gain. _____
ill? _____

Do you re-call that mi-
How man-y days did we

AT THE FIELD OF CLOTH OF GOLD

Lyrics by SHELDON HARNICK

Music by RICHARD RODGERS

AWAY FROM YOU

Lyrics by SHELDON HARNICK

Music by RICHARD RODGERS

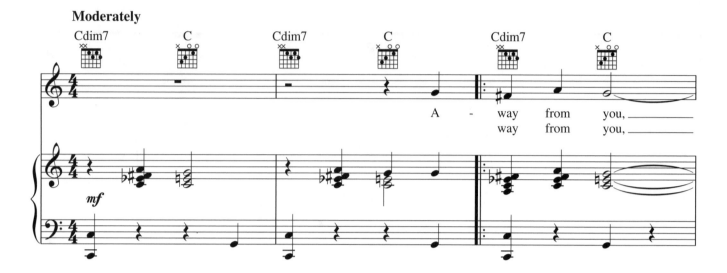

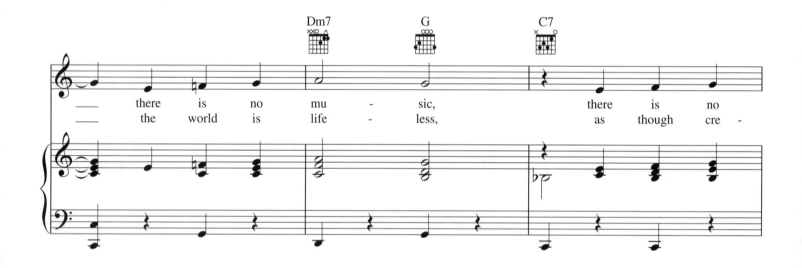

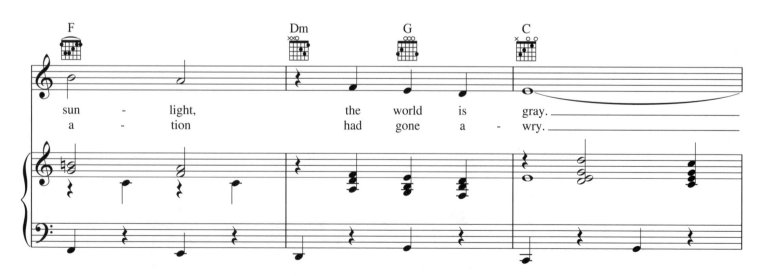

THE CHASE

Lyrics by SHELDON HARNICK

Music by RICHARD RODGERS

ELIZABETH

Lyrics by SHELDON HARNICK

Music by RICHARD RODGERS

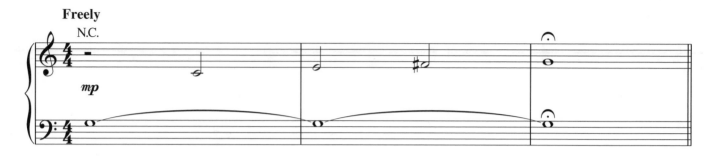

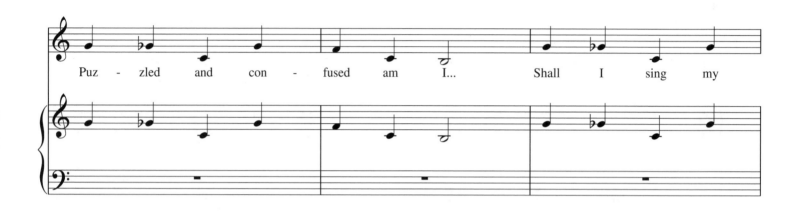

Puz - zled and con - fused am I... Shall I sing my

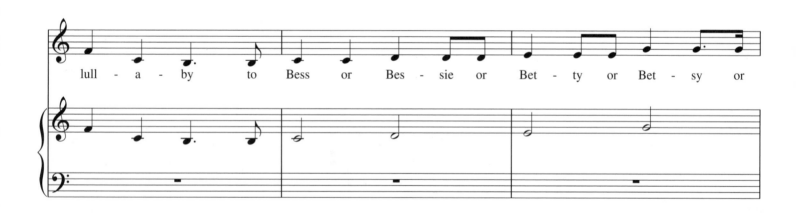

lull - a - by to Bess or Bes - sie or Bet - ty or Bet - sy or

Beth or Liz or Liz - beth or Liz - zie? Please go to sleep. _____

IN TIME

Lyrics by SHELDON HARNICK

Music by RICHARD RODGERS

*These lyrics can be sung outside the context of the show. They are not the show lyrics.

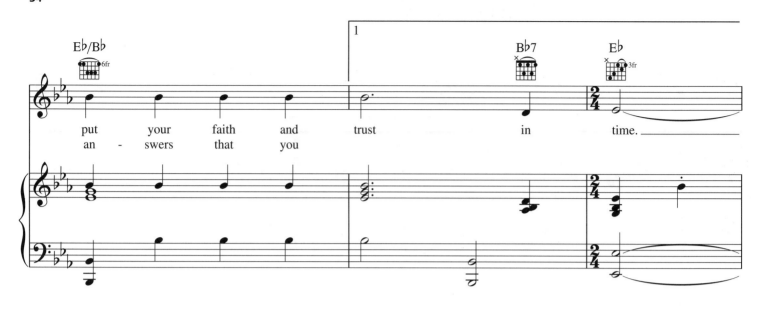

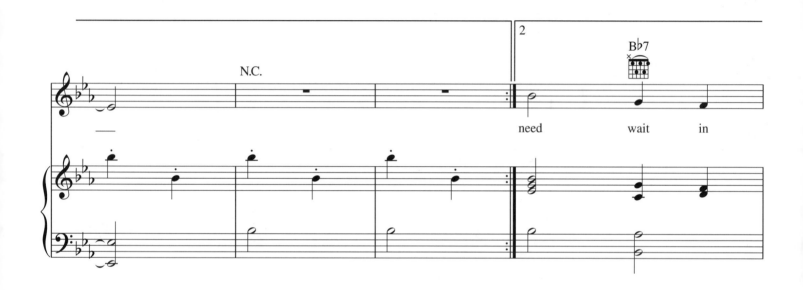

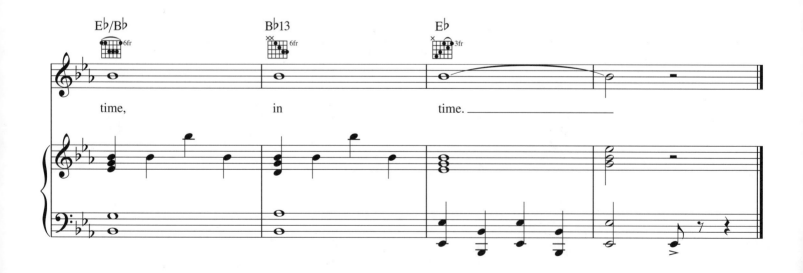

NO SONG MORE PLEASING

Lyrics by SHELDON HARNICK

Music by RICHARD RODGERS

THE PEARS OF ANJOU

Lyrics by SHELDON HARNICK

Music by RICHARD RODGERS

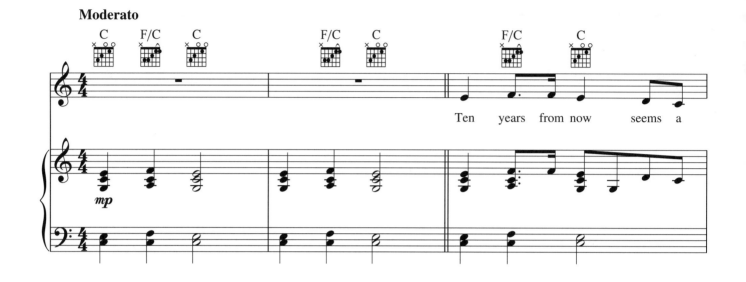

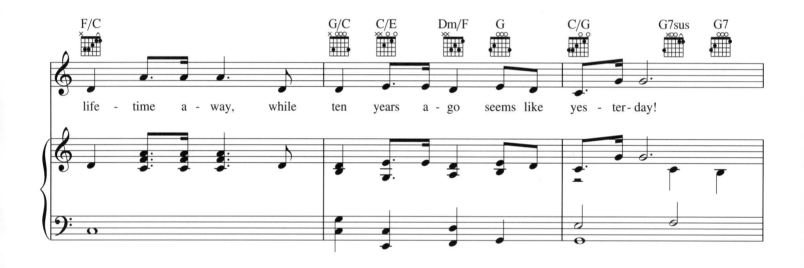

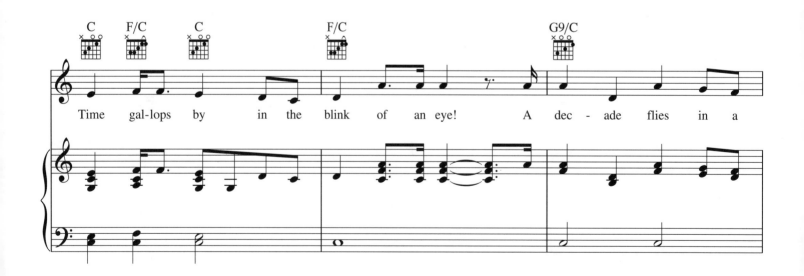

SO MUCH YOU LOVED ME

Lyrics by SHELDON HARNICK

Music by RICHARD RODGERS

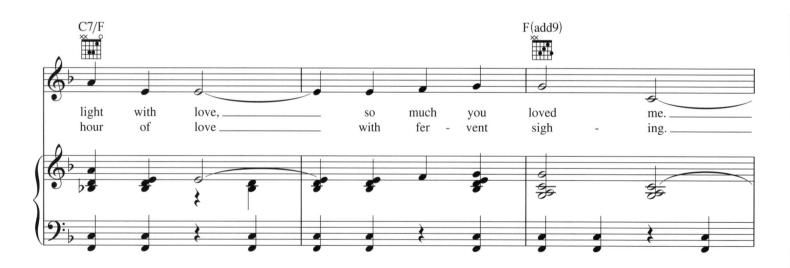

TE DEUM

Lyrics by SHELDON HARNICK

Music by RICHARD RODGERS

TELL ME

Lyrics by SHELDON HARNICK

Music by RICHARD RODGERS

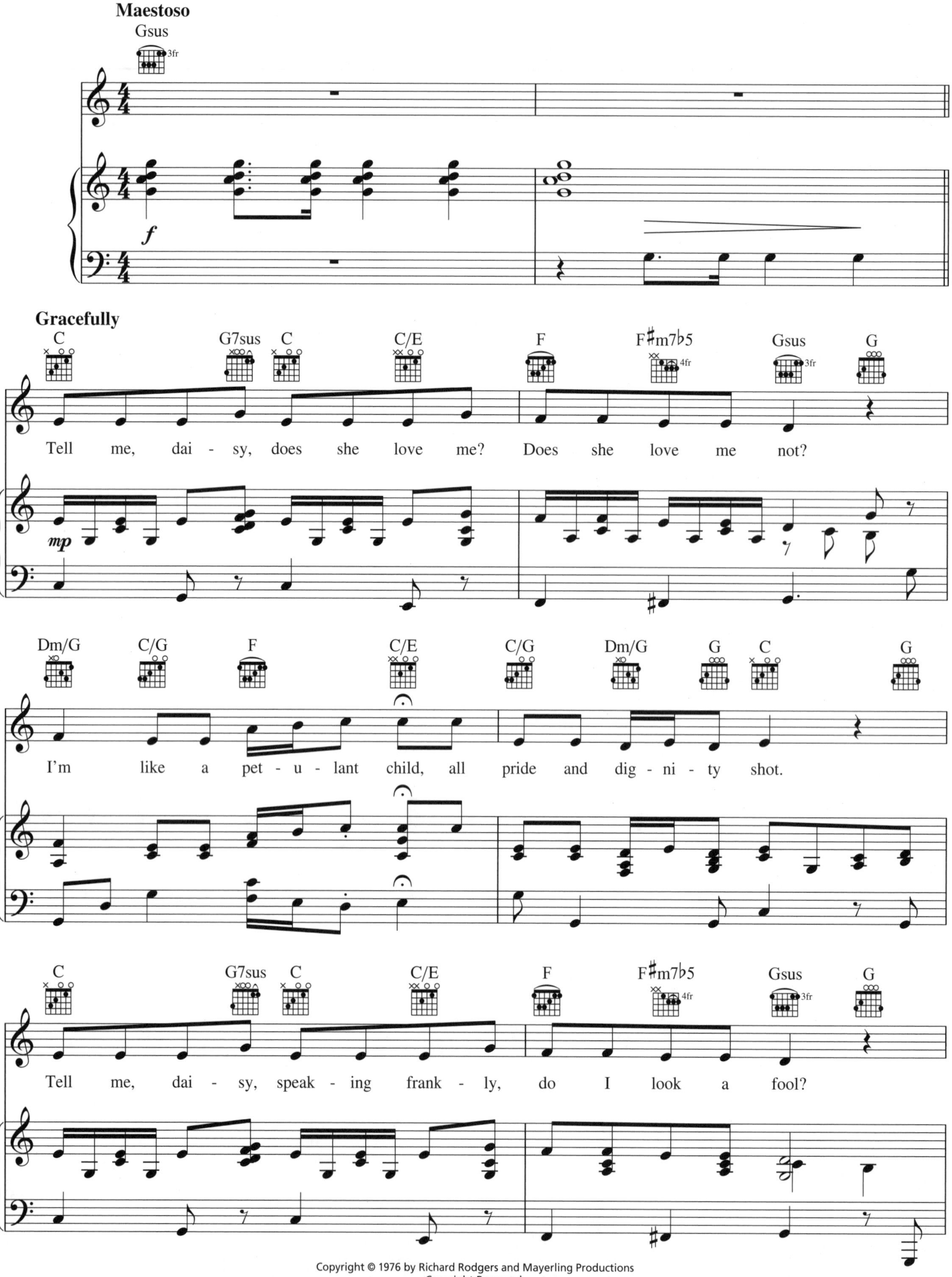

Maestoso
Gsus
3fr
f
Gracefully
C G7sus C C/E F F♯m7♭5 Gsus G
4fr
mp
Tell me, dai - sy, does she love me? Does she love me not?
Dm/G C/G F C/E C/G Dm/G G C G
I'm like a pet - u - lant child, all pride and dig - ni - ty shot.
C G7sus C C/E F F♯m7♭5 Gsus G
Tell me, dai - sy, speak - ing frank - ly, do I look a fool?